Ev
Cant~~onese for~~
parents

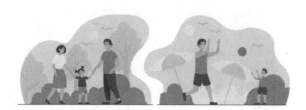

Ann Hamilton

For Ava, Lily and Tom

Further thanks to Sharon Lee, William Lee & Nicole Yip

MESSAGE FROM THE AUTHOR

It wasn't until I became a parent 4 years ago that I realised how much I wanted my children to learn Chinese. Being a first generation British born Chinese (BBC) my parents and grandma raised us to speak Hakka (a dialect of Southern China). I do not regret that one bit as I'll always have that Hakka connection, however sadly it is not commonly spoken these days and as I've gotten older, my Chinese has got rustier. I have struggled many times communicating in Hong Kong and awkwardly reverting to English.

With my basic Cantonese, I soon realised that in order for my children to learn Cantonese, they need to hear me speak it and I need to create a need to communicate in Cantonese. As they say, it starts a home, but living in the UK, far from any Chinese playgroups or schools and my husband not speaking Chinese, the odds are stacked against us.

Being a working mum, with limited time (and energy) I needed something that help will teach me and my family Cantonese while taking care of and playing with them. This is when I thought, why not just slowly convert what I say every day to Cantonese? This was when this book was born.

In this book I have included useful phrases used in everyday life so it will be used repetitvely. This phrasebook is geared towards colloquial Cantonese rather than formal as it's purpose is to teach Cantonese that would be otherwise spoken at home with family and friends.

The aim of this book is to help introduce key vocabulary used in everyday situations and become familiar with the sentence structure used in daily conversation.

With that said, I hope this book makes learning Cantonese for you and your family less intimidating, less stressful and most importantly, fun. My kids find it highly amusing hearing their dad try to speak Chinese!

Good luck and wishing you and your family all the best in your Cantonese journey!

加油! Gaa1 jau2!   (a saying of encouragement, literally meaning - add oil!)

Ann

CONTENTS

The Basics

Daily routine

Health and personal care

Daily activities

Early learning and play

Eating

Social skills & emotions

Sleeping

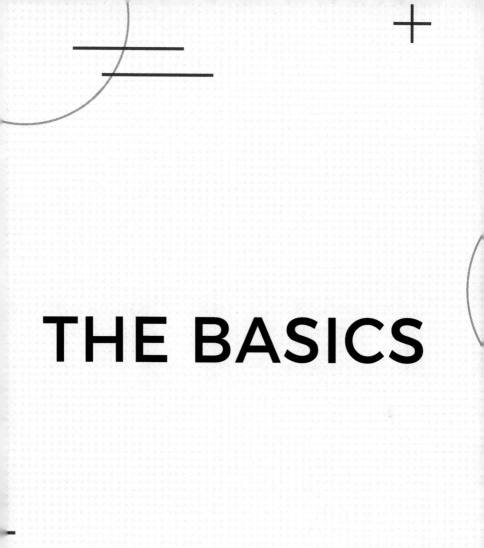

THE BASICS

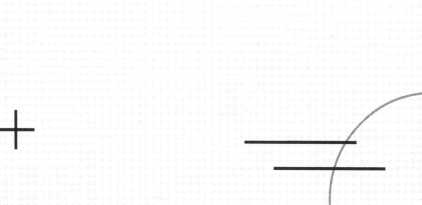

An introduction to the Jyutping romanization system

Romanization is the use of English letters to represent Cantonese syllables. If you are unable to read Chinese characters, you can still read what is written in English. This book uses the Jyutping romanization system (please note this book is also available in Yale romanization).

The Jyutping system was introduced by the Hong Kong Linguistic Society in 1993. Since then, Jyutping has become the norm and most Cantonese learning resources have since adopted this system.

The biggest difference is that the tones are represented with numbers rather than tone marks.

Cantonese is a tonal language and the best way to learn is to listen closely to native speakers and to mimic the sounds they make.

Each syllable of Cantonese is composed of three elements:

Initial + Final + Tone
(Consonants) (Vowels)

Initial
(Consonants)
The **beginning** sound element

Final
(Vowels)
The **ending** sound element

Tone
The relative or variation of **pitch** of a syllable

Initials
There are 19 initials (consonants)

p	b	t	d	k	g	c	ch	j	k w

g w	m	n	n g	f	l	h	s	z

Tricky initials

Jyutping	How it sounds in English
ng	**ung** (silent g)
c	**ts** (as in **ts**unami)
m	**mmm**

Tones
There are 6 distinctive tones in Cantonese.

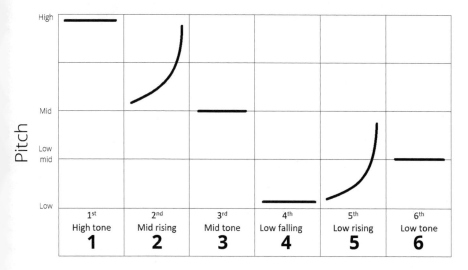

	1st	2nd	3rd	4th	5th	6th
	High tone	Mid rising	Mid tone	Low falling	Low rising	Low tone
	1	**2**	**3**	**4**	**5**	**6**

Tone

Tone 1	High tone
Tone 2	Mid -rising
Tone 3	Mid tone
Tone 4	Low falling
Tone 5	Low rising
Tone 6	Low

Example: si

1st	2nd	3rd	4th	5th	6th
絲 **si1**	史 **si2**	試 **si3**	時 **si4**	市 **si5**	是 **si6**
silk/ thread	history	to test/ try	time/ period	market/ city	yes/to be

BASIC GRAMMAR

Pronouns

I /me	我	Ngo5
You	你	Nei5
He/ she	佢	Keoi5
We/ us	我哋	Ngo5 dei6
You (plural)	你哋	Nei5 dei6
They/ them	佢哋	Keoi5 dei6

Possession

My/ mine	我嘅	Ngo5 ge3
Your/ yours	你嘅	Nei5 ge3
His/ hers	佢嘅	Keoi5 ge3
Our	我哋嘅	Ngo5 dei6 ge3
Yours (plural)	你哋嘅	Nei5 dei6 ge3
Theirs	佢哋嘅	Keoi5 dei6 ge3

Questions

Where?	邊度呀?	Bin1 dou6 aa1?
How?	點樣呀?	Dim2 joeng2 aa1?
Why?	點解呀?	Dim2 gaai2 aa1?
When?	幾時呀?	Gei2 si4 aa1?
Who?	邊個呀?	Bin1 go3 aa1?
What?	乜嘢呀?	Mat1 je5 aa1?

Measure words/ classifiers

Just as you would say two pieces of toast or a pair of shoes, the majority of words come with a classifier in Cantonese. As there isn't a singular or plural form in Chinese, classifiers are used to help quantify an object.

A sentence with a measure word consists of:

A number	**+**	A measure word	**+**	Noun (object)

For example: 3 people 三個人

三	個	人
saam1	go3	jan4
3	**measure word**	**people**

Common classifiers

The list below are some of the common ones with examples in what context they can be used. If you are unsure, a safe bet will be to use 個 *go3* and the majority of people will understand.

個	Go3	The most common: people, round objects, countries & regions, ideas, questions.
杯	Bui1	Cups, glasses
本	Bun2	Books & magazines
隻	Zek3	Mammals, birds, insects
支	Zi1	For long, thin, objects
樽	Zeon1	Bottles
塊	Faai3	Slice, piece
架	Gaa3	Vehicles, cars, plane, computer devices, TV
張	Zoeng1	Flat things such as paper, documents, note bills
首	Sau2	Songs
件	Gin6	For clothes worn on the upper part of the body e.g. shirt
條	Tiu4	For clothes worn on the lower part of the body e.g trousers, leggings. Also long objects e.g string, ribbon, hair , keys

Days of the week

Monday	星期一	Sing1 kei4 jat1
Tuesday	星期二	Sing1 kei4 ji6
Wednesday	星期三	Sing1 kei4 saam1
Thursday	星期四	Sing1 kei4 sei3
Friday	星期五	Sing1 kei4 ng5
Saturday	星期六	Sing1 kei4 luk6
Sunday	星期日	Sing1 kei4 jat6

Months of the year

January	一月	Jat1 jyut6
February	二月	Ji6 jyut6
March	三月	Saam1 jyut6
April	四月	Sei3 jyut6
May	五月	Ng5 jyut6
June	六月	Luk6 jyut6
July	七月	Cat1 jyut6
August	八月	Baat3 jyut6
September	九月	Gau2 jyut6
October	十月	Sap6 jyut6
November	十一月	Sap6 jat1 jyut6
December	十二月	Sap6 ji6 jyut6

DAILY
ROUTINE

1. GOOD MORNING!

早晨！

ZOU2 SAN4!

It's time to wake up!

夠鐘起身喇！

Gau3 zung1 hei2 san1 laa3!

Did you sleep well?

你瞓得好唔好？

Nei5 fan3 dak1 hou2 m4 hou2?

What did you dream about?

你發咗個咩夢呀？

Nei5 faat3 zo2 go3 me1 mung6 aa1?

That's a nice dream!

係好夢嚟㗎！

Hai6 hou2 mung6 lai4 bo3!

Don't worry, it was just a dream.

唔使驚，夢嚟啫。

M4 sai2 geng1, mung6 lai4 ze1.

Let's get ready for the day.

要準備開始新嘅一日啦！

Jiu3 zeon2 bei6 hoi1 ci2 san1 ge3 jat1 jat6 laa1!

You need to get up or we will be late.

你好起身喇，如果唔係我哋就遲到㗎喇。

Nei5 hou2 hei2 san1 laa3, jyu4 gwo2 m4 hai6 ngo5 dei6 zau6 ci4 dou3 gaa3 laa3.

Hurry up!	快啲啦！
	Faai3 di1 laa1!
Put your dressing gown on.	著返件睡袍。
	Zoek3 faan1 gin6 seoi6 pou4.

Vocabulary 詞彙 ci4 wui6

Alarm clock	鬧鐘	Naau6 zung1
Wake up	起身	Hei2 san1
Dream	夢	Mung6
Sleep	瞓覺	Fan3 gaau3
Dressing gown	瞓覺衫	Fan3 gaau3 saam1
To be late	遲到	Ci4 dou3

2. FEEDING BABY
餵食
WAI3 SIK6

Are you hungry? Let mummy feed you?	你肚餓未？等媽咪餵你。 Nei5 tou5 ngo6 mei6? Dang2 maa1 mi4 wai3 nei5.
I'm making a bottle.	我整緊樽奶。 Ngo5 zing2 gan2 zeon1 naai5.
It's coming! Hang on!	嚟緊啦！等陣！ Lai4 gan2 laa1! Dang2 zan6!
Have you finished?	食曬未？ Sik6 saai3 mei6?
Let me burp you.	等我幫你掃風。 Dang2 ngo5 bong1 nei5 sou3 fung1
Wow that's a good burp!	嘩，唔得好大聲！ Waa1, goe1 dak1 hou2 daai6 seng1!

Vocabulary 詞彙 ci4 wui6

Baby formula	嬰兒配方	Jing1 ji4 pui3 fong1
Baby bottle	奶樽	Naai5 zeon1
Breast feeding	餵人奶	Wai3 jan4 naai5
Sippy cup	啜飲杯	Zyut3 jam2 bui1
Baby food	BB食品	Bi bi sik6 ban2
High chair	高腳椅	Gou1 goek3 ji2

3.BREAKFAST
早餐
ZOU2 CAAN1

Breakfast is ready.

早餐準備好啦。

Zou2 caan1 zeon2 bei6 hou2 laa1.

Let's eat breakfast.

食早餐啦。

Sik6 zou2 caan1 laa1.

What do you want to eat?

你想食啲咩?

Nei5 soeng2 sik6 di1 me1?

Do you want to eat...?

你想唔想食...?

Nei5 soeng2 m4 soeng2 sik6...?

It's important to have breakfast.

早餐好緊要㗎。

Zou2 caan1 hou2 gan2 jiu3 gaa3.

Please eat up.

快啲食哂佢。

Faai3 di1 sik6 saai3 keoi5.

Have you had enough?

食飽未?

Sik6 baau2 mei6?

Would you like some more?

仲要唔要多啲?

Zung6 jiu3 m4 jiu3 do1 di1?

Well done! You ate it all!

好叻喎！食得晒！

Hou2 lek1 wo3! Sik6 dak1 saai3!

Okay time to get washed and dressed.

好喇，係時候梳洗著衫。

Hou2 laa3, hai6 si4 hau6 so1 sai2 zoek3 saam1.

Vocabulary 詞彙 ci4 wui6

Cereal	穀類	Guk1 leoi6
Toast	多士	Do1 si2
Jam	果醬	Gwo2 zoeng3
Peanut butter	花生醬	Faa1 sang1 zoeng3
Marmalade	柑橘醬	Gam1 gwat1 zoeng3
Marmite	馬麥醬	Maa5 mak6 zoeng3
Eggs	雞蛋	Gai1 daan2
Scrambled eggs	炒蛋	Caau2 daan2
Fried eggs	煎蛋	Zin1 daan2
Boiled eggs	烚蛋	Saap6 daan2
Poached eggs	流心蛋	Lau4 sam1 daan2
Porridge	餬仔	Wu4 zai2
Congee	粥	Zuk1
Fruit	水果	Seoi2 gwo2

4. BRUSHING TEETH

刷牙

CAAT3 NGAA4

Did you brush your teeth?

刷咗牙未?

Caat3 zo2 ngaa4 mei6?

Brush your teeth.

去刷牙。

Heoi3 caat3 ngaa4.

Let (mummy / daddy) brush your teeth.

等(媽咪/爹哋)幫你刷牙。

Dang2 (maa1 mi4/ de1 di4) bong1 nei5 caat3 ngaa4.

Open your mouth please.

擘大口吖唔該。

Maak3 daai6 hau2 aa1 m4 goi1.

I'll help you brush your teeth.

我幫你刷牙。

Ngo5 bong1 nei5 caat3 ngaa4.

Put some toothpaste on the brush.

吱啲牙膏喺牙刷上面。

Zi1 di1 ngaa4 gou1 hai2 ngaa4 caat2 soeng6 min6.

Don't squirt too much toothpaste.

唔好吱咁多牙膏。

M4 hou2 zi1 gam3 do1 ngaa4 gou1.

Make sure you brush properly.	刷乾淨啲呀。	Caat3 gon1 zing6 di1 aa3.
Spit the water.	㩘咗啲水佢。	Loe1 zo2 di1 seoi2 keoi5.
Remember to floss.	記得用牙線。	Gei3 dak1 jung6 ngaa4 sin3.
Well done!	做得好！	Zou6 dak1 hou2!

Vocabulary 詞彙 ci4 wui6

Toothbrush	牙刷	Ngaa4 caat2
Toothpaste	牙膏	Ngaa4 gou1
Mouthwash	漱口水	Sau3 hau2 seoi2
Electric toothbrush	電動牙刷	Din6 dung6 ngaa4 caat2
Braces	牙套	Ngaa4 tou3
Teeth	牙	Ngaa4
Cavity	蛀牙	Zyu3 ngaa4
Floss	牙線	Ngaa4 sin3

5. GETTING WASHED
梳洗
SO1 SAI2

Wash your face.

去洗臉。
Heoi3 sai2 lim5.

You have sleep in your eye.

你有眼屎。
Nei5 jau5 ngaan5 si2.

You have a bogie, blow your nose in a tissue.

你有鼻屎，用紙巾擦咗佢。
Nei5 jau5 bei6 si2, jung6 zi2 gan1 caat3 zo2 keoi5.

Wash your face with a flannel.

用毛巾洗面。
Jung6 mou4 gan1 sai2 min6.

Roll your sleeves up.

捲起手袖。
Gyun2 hei2 sau2 zau6.

Wash your hands with soap.

用番梘洗手。
Jung6 faan1 gaan2 sai2 sau2.

Rub your hands properly.

好好掂乾淨對手。
Hou2 hou2 zeot1 gon1 zing6 deoi3 sau2.

Rinse all the soap off.

沖乾淨啲番梘佢。
Cung1 gon1 zing6 di1 faan1 gaan2 keoi5.

Do you need any help?	使唔使我幫手？ Sai2 m4 sai2 ngo5 bong1 sau2?	
Is the water too (hot/ cold?)	啲水會唔會太(熱/凍)？ Di1 seoi2 wui5 m4 wui5 taai3 (jit6/ dung3)?	
Don't mess about!	唔好搞搞震！ M4 hou2 gaau2 gaau2 zan3!	
Dry your hands with a towel.	用毛巾抹乾對手。 Jung6 mou4 gan1 maat3 gon1 deoi3 sau2.	
All clean!	乾淨哂！ Gon1 zing6 saai3!	
Go get dressed.	去著衫喇。 Heoi3 zoek3 saam1 laa3.	

Vocabulary 詞彙 ci4 wui6

Bogie	鼻屎	Bei6 si2
Eye boogers / sleep	眼屎	Ngaan5 si2
Tissue	紙巾	Zi2 gan1
Flannel	絨布	Jung2 bou3
Hand	手	Sau2
Eyes	眼	Ngaan5
Face	面	Min6
Soap	番梘	Faan1 gaan2
Tap	水龍頭	Seoi2 lung4 tau4
Towel	毛巾	Mou4 gan1

6. GETTING DRESSED

著衫

ZOEK3 SAAM1

What do you want to wear?	你想著咩衫? Nei5 soeng2 zoek3 me1 saam1?
Do you want this one or this one?	你要呢件定個件呀? Nei5 jiu3 ni1 gin6 ding6 go3 gin6 aa3?
Can you choose something else?	你可唔可以揀其他? Nei5 ho2 m4 ho2 ji5 gaan2 kei4 taa1?
You'll be too hot wearing that.	你著個件會唔會太熱。 Nei5 zoek3 go3 gin6 wui5 m4 wui5 taai3 jit6.
This is too (small / big).	呢件太(細/大)。 Ni1 gin6 taai3 (sai3/ daai6).
How about this?	呢件你覺得點? Ni1 gin6 nei5 gok3 dak1 dim2?
Let me put this on for you.	我幫你著。 Ngo5 bong1 nei5 zoek3.
Lift your arms.	舉高你對手。 Geoi2 gou1 nei5 deoi3 sau2.

Put your arms through here.	將你對手穿過去。 Zoeng1 nei5 deoi3 sau2 cyun1 gwo3 heoi3.
Stand up.	企起身。 Kei5 hei2 san1.
Let me pull this (up/down).	等我拉(高/低)佢。 Dang2 ngo5 laai1 (gou1/ dai1) keoi5.
Stay still please!	唔好亂郁唔該! M4 hou2 lyun6 juk1 m4 goi1!
Do you need any help?	使唔使我幫手? Sai2 m4 sai2 ngo5 bong1 sau2?
It looks good on you!	你著得好好睇! Nei5 zoek3 dak1 hou2 hou2 tai2!
Please hurry up!	快趣啲唔該! Faai3 ceoi3 di1 m4 goi1!
Put your shoes on.	去著鞋。 Heoi3 zoek3 haai4.
Give me your (left/right) foot.	畀你隻(左/右)腳我。 Bei2 nei5 zek3 (zo2/ jau6) goek3 ngo5.
You've got your shoes on the wrong feet!	你對鞋著錯咗喇! Nei5 deoi3 haai4 zoek3 co3 zo2 laa3!

Do you want me to help with the shoelaces?

使唔使我幫手綁鞋帶?

Sai2 m4 sai2 ngo5 bong1 sau2 bong2 haai4 daai2?

Vocabulary 詞彙 ci4 wui6

Clothes	衫	Saam1
T Shirt	T裇	T seot1
Shirt	恤衫	Seot1 saam1
Sweater	冷衫	Laang1 saam1
Vest	背心	Bui3 sam1
Underpants	內褲	Noi6 fu3
Skirt	裙	Kwan4
Shorts	短褲	Dyun2 fu3
Trousers	褲	Fu3
Jeans	牛仔褲	Ngau4 zai2 fu3
Coat	大褸	Daai6 lau1
Rain coat	雨衣	Jyu5 ji1
Jacket	外套	Ngoi6 tou3
Socks	襪	Mat6
Tights	絲襪	Si1 mat6
Sandles	涼鞋	Loeng4 haai4
Slippers	拖鞋	To1 haai2
Shoes	鞋	Haai2
Glasses	眼鏡	Ngaan5 geng2

HEALTH & PERSONAL CARE

7. CHANGING NAPPY
換尿片
WUN6 NIU6 PIN2

Change a nappy.
換片。
Wun6 pin2.

Let me smell.
等我聞吓。
Dang2 ngo5 man4 haa5.

Let me check your nappy.
等我檢查吓你條尿片。
Dang2 ngo5 gim2 caa4 haa5
nei5 tiu4 niu6 pin2.

Wow! We need to change your nappy!
嘩！要換尿布片喇！
Waa1! jiu3 wun6 niu6 bou3
pin2 laa3!

Nappy is still dry.
尿片仲係乾嘅。
Niu6 pin2 zung6 hai6 gon1 ge3.

Nappy is wet.
尿片濕咗。
Niu6 pin2 sap1 zo2.

Pass me the wet wipes.
幫我拎濕紙巾。
Bong1 ngo5 ling1 sap1 zi2 gan1.

Let's clean your bum!
要洗屁股喇！
Jiu3 sai2 pei3 gu2 laa3!

Lie down.	瞓低。	
	Fan3 dai1.	
Keep still please!	唔該唔好亂郁！	
	M4 goi1 m4 hou2 lyun6 juk1!	
Don't touch that, it's dirty.	唔好亂掂，污糟呀。	
	M4 hou2 lyun6 dim6, wu1 zou1 aa1.	
All done!	搞掂！	
	Gaau2 dim6!	
We're running low on nappies.	我哋唔夠尿布片。	
	Ngo5 dei6 m4 gau3 niu6 bou3 pin2.	
Are there any baby changing facilities here?	請問呢度有冇育嬰室?	
	Cing2 man6 ni1 dou6 jau5 mou5 juk6 jing1 sat1?	
Where are the nearest baby changing room?	請問最近嘅育嬰室喺邊度?	
	Cing2 man6 zeoi3 gan6 ge3 juk6 jing1 sat1 hai2 bin1 dou6?	

Vocabulary 詞彙 ci4 wui6

Nappy	尿片	Niu6 pin2
Wet wipes	濕紙巾	Sap1 zi2 gan1
Nappy cream	護臀霜	Wu6 tyun4 soeng1
Changing mat	換片墊	Wun6 pin2 zin3
Nappy rash	尿疹	Niu6 can2
Changing bag	尿布袋	Niu6 bou3 doi2

8. POTTY TRAINING
如廁訓練
JYU4 CI3 FAN3 LIN6

We're using the potty because you're a big (girl/boy) now.

大個(女/仔)喇，我哋用廁所仔。

Daai6 go3 (neoi5/ zai2) laa3, ngo5 dei6 jung6 ci3 so2 zai2.

Do you need to go on the potty?

你要唔要坐廁所仔呀？

Nei5 jiu3 m4 jiu3 co5 ci3 so2 zai2 aa3?

Do you need a wee or a poo?

你要屙味味定屙唔唔呀？

Nei5 jiu3 o1 zyu3 zyu3 ding6 o1 m4 m4 aa3?

Stay on the potty till you're done.

未屙完之前唔准離開個廁所仔。

Mei6 o1 jyun4 zi1 cin4 m4 zeon2 lei4 hoi1 go3 ci3 so2 zai2.

Well done you did a wee/poo!

好叻喎，屙咗味味/唔唔！

Hou2 lek1 wo3, o1 zo2 zyu3 zyu3/ m4 m4!

Flush the toilet.

嚟沖廁。

Lai4 cung1 ci3.

Pull your trousers up.

著好條褲。

Zoek3 hou2 tiu4 fu3.

9. GOING TO THE TOILET
去廁所
HEOI3 CI3 SO2

Do you need the toilet?

你要唔要去廁所?

Nei5 jiu3 m4 jiu3 heoi3 ci3 so2?

Please go now before we go out.

你而家去咗我哋先出街。

Nei5 ji4 gaa1 heoi3 zo2 ngo5 dei6 sin1 ceot1 gaai1.

Can you hold it?

你忍唔忍到?

Nei5 jan2 m4 jan2 dou3?

We need to find a toilet.

我哋要揾個廁所。

Ngo5 dei6 jiu3 wan2 go3 ci3 so2

Toilet is occupied.

個廁所有人。

Go3 ci3 so2 jau5 jan4.

Do you need me to wipe you?

使唔使我幫你抹?

Sai2 m4 sai2 ngo5 bong1 nei5 maat3?

You can do it all by yourself! Well done!

你自己一個搞得掂喎!好叻叻!

Nei5 zi6 gei2 jat1 go3 gaau2 dak1 dim6 wo3! Hou2 lek1 lek1!

Remember to flush the toilet.	記得要沖廁。	
	Gei3 dak1 jiu3 cung1 ci3.	
Wash your hands well.	洗乾淨對手。	
	Sai2 gon1 zing6 deoi3 sau2.	
Dry your hands.	抹乾對手。	
	Maat3 gon1 deoi3 sau2.	

Vocabulary 詞彙 ci4 wui6

Potty	便盆	Bin6 pun4
Toilet	廁所	Ci3 so2
Toilet paper	廁紙	Ci3 zi2
Paper hand towel	手紙	Sau2 zi2
Seat reducer	兒童廁板	Ji4 tung4 ci3 baan2
Toilet seat	廁所板	Ci3 so2 baan2
Hand dryer	烘乾機	Hong3 gon1 gei1
To flush	沖廁	Cung1 ci3
Soap	番梘	Faan1 gaan2

10. BATH TIME
沖涼
CUNG1 LEONG4

It's bath time!
夠鐘沖涼喇！
Gau3 zung1 cung1 loeng4 laa3!

I'll help you get undressed.
等我幫你除衫。
Dang2 ngo5 bong1 nei5 ceoi4 saam1

Get in the bathtub.
入去浴缸啦。
Jap6 heoi3 juk6 gong1 laa1.

Is it too hot?
會唔會太熱？
Wui5 m4 wui5 taai3 jit6?

Look at the bubbles!
睇吓幾多泡泡！
Tai2 haa5 gei2 do1 pou5 pou5!

Don't splash!
唔好濺到啲水周圍都係！
M4 hou2 zin3 dou3 di1 seoi2 zau1 wai4 dou1 hai6!

Let me wash you.
我幫你沖涼。
Ngo5 bong1 nei5 cung1 loeng4 .

To wash hair.
洗頭。
Sai2 tau4.

Rinse the bubbles off.
沖走啲泡泡。
Cung1 zau2 di1 pou5 pou5.

Are you ready to get out? 出得嚟未?

Ceot1 dak1 lai4 mei6?

Dry yourself. 抹乾個身。

Maat3 gon1 go3 san1.

Dry your hair. 吹頭。

Ceoi1 tau4.

Comb your hair. 梳頭。

So1 tau4.

Put your pyjamas on. 著返套睡衣。

Zoek3 faan1 tou3 seoi6 ji1.

Get ready for bed. 準備瞓覺。

Zeon2 bei6 fan3 gaau3.

Cutting nails 剪指甲 zin2 zi2 gaap3

Wow! Your nails are long! 嘩! 你啲指甲好長!

Waa1! Nei5 di1 zi2 gaap3 hou2 coeng4!

Don't worry, I won't hurt you. 唔使驚, 我唔會整親你。

M4 sai2 geng1, ngo5 m4 wui5 zing2 can1 nei5.

See, it didn't hurt at all! 睇吓, 一啲都唔痛!

Tai2 haa5, jat1 di1 dou1 m4 tung3!

Brushing hair 梳頭 so1 tau4

Your hair needs brushing.	你要梳吓個頭喇。 Nei5 jiu3 so1 haa5 go3 tau4 laa3.
Let me brush your hair.	等我幫你梳頭。 Dang2 ngo5 bong1 nei5 so1 tau4.
Stay still.	唔好郁。 M4 hou2 juk1.
Do you want me to put your hair up in a ponytail?	使唔使我幫你紮返個馬尾? Sai2 m4 sai2 ngo5 bong1 nei5 zaat3 faan1 go3 maa5 mei5?

Vocabulary 詞彙 ci4 wui6

Bath tub	浴缸	Juk6 gong1
Shower	淋浴	Lam4 juk6
Shampoo	洗頭水	Sai2 tau4 seoi2
Soap	番梘	Faan1 gaan2
Towel	毛巾	Mou4 gan1
Comb	梳	So1
Hair clip	髮挾	Faat3 haap6
Nail clippers	指甲鉗	Zi2 gaap3 kim2

11. FEELING UNWELL
唔舒服
M4 SYU1 FUK6

Oh dear, you don't look well!
哎吔，你好似唔舒服！
Aai1 jaa1, nei5 hou2 ci5 m4 syu1 fuk6!

What's wrong?
發生咩事？
Faat3 sang1 me1 si6?

Where does it hurt?
邊度痛？
Bin1 dou6 tung3?

You have a fever.
你發燒啊。
Nei5 faat3 siu1 aa1.

You have a cold.
你感冒啊。
Nei5 gam2 mou6 aa1.

You need some medicine.
你要食藥。
Nei5 jiu3 sik6 joek6.

Drink plenty of water.
飲多啲水。
Jam2 do1 di1 seoi2.

Have some rest.
休息吓。
Jau1 sik1 haa5.

Do you want a cuddle?   要唔要攬攬?

Jiu3 m4 jiu3 laam5 laam5?

Are you feeling better?   感覺有冇好啲?

Gam2 gok3 jau5 mou5 hou2 di1?

Vocabulary 詞彙 ci4 wui6

Tummy ache	肚仔痛	Tou5 zai2 tung3
Headache	頭痛	Tau4 tung3
Toothache	牙痛	Ngaa4 tung3
Runny nose	流鼻水	Lau4 bei6 seoi2
Blocked nose	鼻塞	Bei6 sak1
Sore throat	喉嚨痛	Hau4 lung4 tung3
Cough	咳	Kat1
Fever	發燒	Faat3 siu1
Cold	感冒	Gam2 mou6
Chicken pox	水痘	Seoi2 dau6
Band aid	膠布	Gaau1 bou3

12. THE BODY
身體
SAN1 TAI2

We feel with our hands.
我哋用手摸嘢。
Ngo5 dei6 jung6 sau2 mo2 je5.

We smell with our nose.
我哋用鼻聞嘢。
Ngo5 dei6 jung6 bei6 man4 je5.

We look with our eyes.
我地用眼睇嘢。
Ngo5 dei6 jung6 ngaan5 tai2 je5.

We hear with our ears.
我地用耳仔聽嘢。
Ngo5 dei6 jung6 ji5 zai2 teng1 je5.

We taste with our tongue.
我地用脷試味。
Ngo5 dei6 jung6 lei6 si3 mei6.

Vocabulary 詞彙 ci4 wui6

Arm	手臂	Sau2 bei3
Back	背脊	Bui3 zik3
Chest	心口	Sam1 hau2
Chin	下巴	Haa6 baa1
Ear	耳仔	Ji5 zai2
Eye	眼睛	Ngaan5 zing1
Eyelid	眼皮	Ngaan5 pei4

Face	面	Min6
Feet	腳	Goek3
FIngers	手指	Sau2 zi2
Finger nail	手指甲	Sau2 zi2 gaap3
Hair	頭髮	Tau4 faat3
Hand	手	Sau2
Head	頭	Tau4
Heart	心	Sam1
Leg	腳	Goek3
Lips	嘴唇	Zeoi2 seon4
Mouth	口	Hau2
Neck	頸	Geng2
Nose	鼻子	Bei6 zi2
Shoulder	膊頭	Bok3 tau4
Teeth	牙	Ngaa4
Tongue	脷	Lei6

DAILY ACTIVITIES

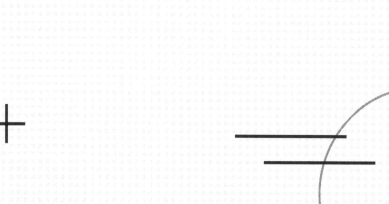

13. WHAT SHALL WE DO TODAY?
今日做啲咩？
GAM1 JAT6 ZOU6 DI1 ME1?

What do you want to do today?
你今日想做啲咩？
Nei5 gam1 jat6 soeng2 zou6 di1 me1?

The weather is nice, let's go out!
天氣咁好，我哋出街啦！
Tin1 hei3 gam3 hou2, ngo5 dei6 ceot1 gaai1 laa1!

Let's go for a walk.
我哋去行吓。
Ngo5 dei6 heoi3 hang4 haa5.

Let's go to the ...
我哋去...
Ngo5 dei6 heoi3...

Let's have a picnic.
我哋去野餐。
Ngo5 dei6 heoi3 je5 caan1.

The weather is bad, let's stay in.
天氣唔好，我哋都係留喺屋企啦。
Tin1 hei3 m4 hou2, ngo5 dei6 dou1 hai6 lau4 hai2 uk1 kei2 laa

Are you feeling tired?
你係咪攰喇？
Nei5 hai6 mai6 gui6 laa3?

Would you rather stay here today?	你今日係咪寧願留喺度?	Nei5 gam1 jat6 hai6 mai6 ning4 jyun2 lau4 hai2 dou6?
Mummy/ daddy is going to work now.	媽咪/爹哋而家返工喇。	Maa1 mi4/ de1 di4 ji4 gaa1 faan1 gung1 laa3.
Give them a kiss please.	錫吓佢地啦。	Sek3 haa5 keoi5 dei6 laa1.

Vocabulary 詞彙 ci4 wui6

Walk	行	Hang4
Stroller	BB車	BB ce1
Park	公園	Gung1 jyun2
Swimming pool	游泳池	Jau4 wing6 ci4
Library	圖書館	Tou4 syu1 gun2
Indoor soft play	柔軟遊樂區	Jau4 jyun5 jau4 lok6 keoi1
Zoo	動物園	Dung6 mat6 jyun4
Cinema	戲院	Hei3 jyun2

14. THE WEATHER
天氣
TIN1 HEI3

What's the weather like today?

今日天氣點?

Gam1 jat6 tin1 hei3 dim2?

Today it's...

今日...

Gam1 jat6 ...

Today the weather is nice.

今日天氣好好。

Gam1 jat6 tin1 hei3 hou2 hou2.

It's so cold!

天氣好凍!

Tin1 hei3 hou2 dung3!

It's so hot!

天氣好熱!

Tin1 hei3 hou2 jit6!

You need to drink plenty of water.

你要飲多啲水。

Nei5 jiu3 jam2 do1 di1 seoi2.

You need to put a hat on.

你要戴返頂帽。

Nei5 jiu3 daai3 faan1 ding2 mou6.

It's too (hot/cold), come inside!

天氣咁(熱/凍),入嚟喇!

Tin1 hei3 gam3 (jit6/ dung3), jap6 lai4 laa3!

Vocabulary 詞彙 ci4 wui6

Sunny	好好太陽	Hou2 hou2 taai3 joeng4
Windy	有風	Jau5 fung1
Hot	熱	Jit6
Cold	凍	Dung3
Warm	暖	Nyun5
Foggy	有霧	Jau5 mou6
Cloudy	陰天	Jam1 tin1
Thunder and lightning	行雷閃電	Haang4 leoi4 sim2 din6
Snowing	落緊雪	Lok6 gan2 syut3
Storm	暴雨	Bou6 jyu5
Spring	春天	Ceon1 tin1
Summer	夏天	Haa6 tin1
Autumn	秋天	Cau1 tin1
Winter	冬天	Dung1 tin1

15. IN THE CAR
喺車裏面
HAI2 CE1 LEOI5 MIN6

Time to go.	夠鐘走喇。 Gau3 zung1 zau2 laa3.
Let's get in the car.	上車。 Soeng5 ce1.
Let me fasten your seatbelt.	等我幫你攬好安全帶。 Dang2 ngo5 bong1 nei5 laam5 hou2 on1 cyun4 daai3.
Please stay still.	唔好郁嚟郁去。 M4 hou2 juk1 lai4 juk1 heoi3.
Put on your seatbelt.	攬好安全帶。 Laam5 hou2 on1 cyun4 daai3.
Do you want to listen to some music?	想唔想聽啲音樂? Soeng2 m4 soeng2 teng1 di1 jam1 ngok6?
We're almost there.	我哋就到喇。 Ngo5 dei6 zau6 dou3 laa3.

I can't help you right now, I'm driving!	我揸緊車，幫唔到你住呀！ Ngo5 zaa1 gan2 ce1, bong1 m4 dou2 nei5 zyu6 aa3!	

I can't help you right now, I'm driving!   我揸緊車，幫唔到你住呀！

Ngo5 zaa1 gan2 ce1, bong1 m4 dou2 nei5 zyu6 aa3!

Sit still.   坐定定。

Co5 ding6 ding6.

Do you feel sick?   你係咪唔舒服？

Nei5 hai6 mai6 m4 syu1 fuk6?

Do you want me to open the window?   使唔使我開個窗？

Sai2 m4 sai2 ngo5 hoi1 go3 coeng1?

Are you too (hot/cold)?   你係咪太(熱/凍)？

Nei5 hai6 mai6 taai3 (jit6/ dung3)?

Stop messing around!   咪搞搞震！

Mai5 gaau2 gaau2 zan3!

Vocabulary 詞彙 ci4 wui6

Car	車	Ce1
Baby car seat	BB安全座椅	BB on1 cyun4 zo6 ji2
Seat belt	安全帶	On1 cyun4 daai3
Radio	電台	Din6 toi4
Motion sickness	暈浪	Wan4 long6

16. VISITING FRIENDS
探 朋 友
TAAM3 PANG4 JAU5

Do you want to play with your friend?

你想唔想同你朋友玩呀?
Nei5 soeng2 m4 soeng2 tung4 nei5 pang4 jau5 waan2 aa3?

What do you want to play?

你想玩啲咩?
Nei5 soeng2 waan2 di1 me1?

Does your friend want to play with this?

你朋友想唔想玩呢個呀?
Nei5 pang4 jau5 soeng2 m4 soeng2 waan2 ni1 go3 aa3?

Remember to share.

記得一齊分享。
Gei3 dak1 jat1 cai4 fan1 hoeng2

Take it in turns.

輪流玩啦。
Leon4 lau2 waan2 laa1.

Give it back to him/her.

畀返佢。
Bei2 faan1 keoi5.

Play nicely.

要好好哋玩。
Jiu3 hou2 hou2 dei2 waan2.

Isn't it fun?	好唔好玩呀?	
	Hou2 m4 hou2 waan2 aa3?	
Who is your best friend?	邊個係你死黨啊?	
	Bin1 go3 hai6 nei5 sei2 dong2 aa1?	

Vocabulary 詞彙 ci4 wui6

Friend	朋友	Pang4 jau5
Best friend	死黨	Sei2 dong2

17. SCHOOL
學校
HOK6 HAAU6

Have you got your school bag packed?

執咗書包未?

Zap1 zo2 syu1 baau1 mei6?

Have you got your P.E. kit / gym bag?

帶咗個運動袋未?

Daai3 zo2 go3 wan6 dung6 doi6 mei6?

Have you done your homework?

啲功課做晒未?

Di1 gung1 fo3 zou6 saai3 mei6?

Do you need any help?

使唔使我幫手?

Sai2 m4 sai2 ngo5 bong1 sau2?

Hurry up or you will miss the bus!

嗱嗱聲，如果唔係走架巴士走喫喇!

Naa4 naa4 seng1, jyu4 gwo2 m4 hai6 zau2 gaa3 baa1 si2 zau2 gaa3 laa3!

Do you need a lift to school?

使唔使車你返學?

Sai2 m4 sai2 ce1 nei5 faan1 hok6

Are there any messages from your teacher?

你老師有冇咩通告?

Nei5 lou5 si1 jau5 mou5 me1 tung1 gou3?

How was school today?	今日學校點呀?
	Gam1 jat6 hok6 haau6 dim2 aa3?
What did you have for lunch?	你午餐食咗啲咩?
	Nei5 ng5 caan1 sik6 zo2 di1 me1?

Vocabulary 詞彙 ci4 wui6

School	學校	Hok6 haau6
School bag	書包	Syu1 baau1
Pencil case	筆袋	Bat1 doi6
School uniform	校服	Haau6 fuk6
Homework	功課	Gung1 fo3
Teacher	老師	Lou5 si1
Headteacher/ principal	校長	Haau6 zoeng2
Classroom	課室	Fo3 sat1

18. HOUSEWORK
家務
GAA1 MOU6

Sweep the floor.　　掃地。
Sou3 dei6.

It's so dusty!　　好多塵呀！
Hou2 do1 can4 aa3!

Mop the floor.　　抹地布。
Maat3 dei6 bou3.

Do the dishes.　　洗碗。
Sai2 wun2.

Clear the table.　　執枱。
Zap1 toi2.

Tidy up the room.　　執房。
Zap1 fong2.

Make the bed.　　執床。
Zap1 cong4.

Friends are coming, hurry tidy up the house!　　有朋友嚟，快啲執屋啦！
Jau5 pang4 jau5 lai4, faai3 di1 zap1 uk1 laa1!

Put that in the bin.	抌佢落垃圾桶。	
	Dam2 keoi5 lok6 laap6 saap3 tung2.	
Take out the rubbish.	揼垃圾。	
	Dam2 laap6 saap3.	
Can you help me?	你可唔可以幫我?	
	Nei5 ho2 m4 ho2 ji5 bong1 ngo5?	

Vocabulary 詞彙 ci4 mui6

Rubbish	垃圾	Laap6 saap3
Bin	垃圾桶	Laap6 saap3 tung2
Tidy	執	Zap1
Wash	洗	Sai2
Sweep	掃	Sou3

EARLY
LEARNING &
PLAY

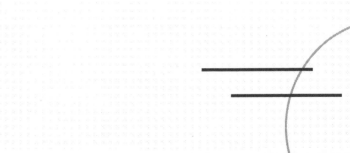

19. EARLY LEARNING

學前教育

HOK6 CIN4 GAAU3 JUK6

Numbers 數字 sou3 zi6

Let's count to 10 in Cantonese.	我哋用廣東話數到十。 Ngo5 dei6 jung6 gwong2 dung1 waa2 sou3 dou3 sap6.
Repeat after me.	跟住我讀。 Gan1 zyu6 ngo5 duk6.
What number is this?	呢個係咩數字? Ni1 go3 hai6 me1 sou3 zi6?
Correct!	啱啦! Ngaam1 laa1!
Try again.	再試一次。 Zoi3 si3 jat1 ci3.
Can you count to 10?	你可唔可以數到十? Nei5 ho2 m4 ho2 ji5 sou3 dou2 sap6?
How many ... can you see?	你見到有幾多個......? Nei5 gin3 dou2 jau5 gei2 do1 go3......?

0	零	Ling4
1	一	Jat1
2	二	Ji6
3	三	Saam1
4	四	Sei3
5	五	Ng5
6	六	Luk6
7	七	Cat1
8	八	Baat3
9	九	Gau2
10	十	Sap6
21	二十一	Ji6 sap6 jat1
100	一百	Jat1 baak3
1000	一千	Jat1 cin1

First	第一	Dai6 jat1
Second	第二	Dai6 ji6
Third	第三	Dai6 saam1
Fourth	第四	Dai6 sei3

Once	一次	Jat1 ci3
Twice	兩次	Loeng5 ci3
Three times	三次	Saam1 ci3

Colours 顏色 ngaan4 sik1

Let's learn colours!
我哋嚟學顏色!
Ngo5 dei6 lai4 hok6 ngaan4 sik1!

What colour is this?
呢個係咩色?
Ni1 go3 hai6 me1 sik1?

What is your favourite colour?
你最鍾意咩色?
Nei5 zeoi3 zung1 ji3 me1 sik1?

Colour this picture in.
你嚟幫張圖填色。
Nei5 lai4 bong1 zoeng1 tou4 tin4 sik1.

Find something that is red.
搵啲紅色嘅嘢。
Wan2 di1 hung4 sik1 ge3 je5.

Red	紅色	Hung4 sik1
Orange	橙色	Caang2 sik1
Yellow	黃色	Wong4 sik1
Green	綠色	Luk6 sik1
Blue	藍色	Laam4 sik1
Purple	紫色	Zi2 sik1
Pink	粉紅色	Fan2 hung4 sik1
White	白色	Baak6 sik1
Gray	灰色	Fui1 sik1
Black	黑色	Hak1 sik1

Let's learn shapes!	我哋嚟學形狀！	
	Ngo5 dei6 lai4 hok6 jing4 zong6!	
What shape is this?	呢個係咩形狀？	
	Ni1 go3 hai6 me1 jing4 zong6?	
How many sides does it have?	佢有幾多條邊？	
	Keoi5 jau5 gei2 do1 tiu4 bin1?	
Can you draw it?	你可唔可以畫佢出嚟？	
	Nei5 ho2 m4 ho2 ji5 waak6 keoi5 ceot1 lai4?	

Circle	圓形	Jyun4 jing4
Triangle	三角形	Saam1 gok3 jing4
Square	方形	Fong1 jing4
Rectangle	長方形	Coeng4 fong1 jing4
Pentagon	五邊形	Ng5 bin1 jing4
Hexagon	六邊形	Luk6 bin1 jing4
Oval	橢圓形	To5 jyun4 jing4
Cube	立方體	Lap6 fong1 tai2
Sphere	球體	Kau4 tai2
Cylinder	圓筒	Jyun4 tung4

What is this?	呢樣係咩嚟㗎?	
	Ni1 joeng6 hai6 me1 lai4 gaa3?	
What does it taste like?	佢食落係咩味?	
	Keoi5 sik6 lok6 hai6 me1 mei6?	
Is it sweet?	佢甜嗎?	
	Keoi5 tim4 maa3?	
Is it sour?	佢酸嗎?	
	Keoi5 syun1 maa3?	
Do you like them?	你鍾唔鍾意食?	
	Nei5 zung1 m4 zung1 ji3 sik6?	

Apple	蘋果	Ping4 gwo2
Banana	香蕉	Hoeng1 ziu1
Carrot	紅蘿蔔	Hung4 lo4 baak6
Cucumber	青瓜	Cing1 gwaa1
Grapes	提子	Tai4 zi2
Lemon	檸檬	Ning4 mung1
Lettuce	生菜	Saang1 coi3
Orange	橙	Caang2
Pear	梨	Lei4
Pineapple	菠蘿	Bo1 lo4
Potato	薯仔	Syu4 zai2
Strawberry	士多啤梨	Si6 do1 pai5 lei4

Animals 動物 dung6 mat6

What animal is this?	呢隻係咩動物?
	Ni1 zek3 hai6 me1 dung6 mat6?
What noise does it make?	佢啲叫聲係點㗎?
	Keoi5 di1 giu3 seng1 hai6 dim2 gaa3?
Where does it live?	佢住喺邊度?
	Keoi5 zyu6 hai2 bin1 dou6?
What does it eat?	佢平時食啲咩㗎?
	Keoi5 ping4 si4 sik6 di1 me1 gaa3
Can you draw a rabbit?	你可唔可以畫隻兔仔出嚟?
	Nei5 ho2 m4 ho2 ji5 waak6 zek3 tou3 zai2 ceot1 lai4?

Cat	貓	Maau1
Dog	狗	Gau2
Fish	魚	Jyu4
Rabbit	兔	Tou3
Hamster	倉鼠	Cong1 syu2
Cow	牛	Ngau4
Horse	馬	Maa5
Sheep	羊	Joeng4
Chicken	雞	Gai1
Pig	豬	Zyu1

20. PLAYING WITH TOYS
玩玩具
WAAN2 WAAN2 GEOI6

Building blocks 積木 zik1 muk6

What do you want to play?	你想玩啲咩？ Nei5 soeng2 waan2 di1 me1?
Let's build a house.	我哋嚟砌間屋。 Ngo5 dei6 lai4 cai3 gaan1 uk1.
Can you put this here?	你可唔可以放佢喺呢度？ Nei5 ho2 m4 ho2 ji5 fong3 keoi5 hai2 ni1 dou6?
Stack the bricks.	疊起啲積木。 Dip6 hei2 di1 zik1 muk6.
Oh no! It fell over!	哎吔！冧咗喇！ Aai1 jaa1! Lam1 zo2 laa3!
Can you find a (red) brick?	你搵唔搵到舊（紅色）積木？ Nei5 wan2 m4 wan2 dou3 gau6 (hung4 sik1) zik1 muk6?
What are you making?	你喺度砌緊啲咩呀？ Nei5 hai2 dou6 cai3 gan2 di1 me1 aa3?
That's really cool!	好勁喎！ Hou2 ging6 wo3!

Puzzles 砌圖 cai3 tou4

Where does that piece go?	嗰塊應該放邊㗎? Go2 faai3 jing1 goi1 fong3 bin1 gaa3?
Does that fit?	啱唔啱㗎? Ngaam1 m4 ngaam1 gaa3?
I don't think it fits.	好似唔係好啱喎。 Hou2 ci5 m4 hai6 hou2 ngaam1 wo3
Try again.	再試多次。 Zoi3 si3 do1 ci3.
Yes, you've got it!	係喇,咁就啱喇! Hai6 laa3, gam2 zau6 ngaam1 laa3!

Drawing 畫畫 waak6 waa2

Let's draw with crayons.	我哋用蠟筆。 Ngo5 dei6 jung6 laap6 bat1.
What are you drawing?	你喺度畫緊啲咩呀? Nei5 hai2 dou6 waak6 gan2 di1 me1 aa3?
Don't draw on the wall!	唔好畫喺牆上面! M4 hou2 waak6 hai2 coeng4 soeng6 min6!
Wow! That's great!	嘩! 畫得好靚喎! Waa1! Waak6 dak1 hou2 leng3 wo3

Play dough 玩黏土　waan2 nim1 tou2

Roll the play dough.　搓吓啲泥膠。

Co1 haa5 di1 nai4 gaau1.

Cut it.　切吓佢。

Cit3 haa5 keoi5.

Squash it.　撳扁佢。

Gam6 bin2 keoi5.

What are you making?　你喺度整緊啲咩呀?

Nei5 hai2 dou6 zing2 gan2 di1 me1 aa3?

Painting 油漆　jau4 cat1

What are you painting?　你喺度畫緊啲咩呀?

Nei5 hai2 dou6 waak6 gan2 di1 me1 aa3?

Try not to be too messy!　盡量唔好整到周圍亂七八糟啦!

Zeon6 loeng4 m4 hou2 zing2 dou3 zau1 wai4 lyun6 cat1 baat3 zou1 laa1!

What happens when you mix the colours?　啲顏色溝埋會變咩色?

Di1 ngaan4 sik1 kau1 maai4 wui6 bin3 me1 sik1?

Let it dry.　晾乾佢。

Long6 gon1 keoi5.

Let's play together.	我哋一齊玩吖。	
	Ngo5 dei6 jat1 cai4 waan2 aa1.	
Wait your turn.	等陣輪到你。	
	Dang2 zan6 leon4 dou3 nei5.	
Good idea!	好主意!	
	Hou2 zyu2 ji3!	
Please share.	同人一齊玩。	
	Tung4 jan4 jat1 cai4 waan2.	
This is fun!	好好玩!	
	Hou2 hou2 waan2!	
It's time to tidy up.	執返好啲嘢喇。	
	Zap1 faan1 hou2 di1 je5 laa3.	

Vocabulary 詞彙 ci4 wui6

Toy blocks	積木	Zik1 muk6
Colouring book	填色書	Tin4 sik1 syu1
Colouring pencils	顏色筆	Ngaan4 sik1 bat1
Felt tip pens	水筆畫畫	Seoi2 bat1 waak6 waa2
Paint brush	畫筆	Waak6 bat1
Paint	漆	Cat1
Toy toy train	玩具火車	Wun6 geoi6 fo2 ce1
Skipping rope	跳繩	Tiu3 sing2
Stuffed toy	毛公仔	Mou4 gung1 zai2
Toy box	玩具箱	Wun6 geoi6 soeng1

21. READING TOGETHER
一齊睇書
JAT1 CAI4 TAI2 SYU1

Let's read a book together.
我哋一齊睇書。
Ngo5 dei6 jat1 cai4 tai2 syu1.

Pick a book you want to read.
揀本你想睇嘅書吖。
Gaan2 bun2 nei5 soeng2 tai2 ge3 syu1 aa1.

How about this one?
不如呢本?
Bat1 jyu4 ni1 bun2?

Do you want me to read to you?
想唔想我讀俾你聽?
Soeng2 m4 soeng2 ngo5 duk6 bei2 nei5 teng1?

Let's read together.
我哋一齊睇。
Ngo5 dei6 jat1 cai4 tai2.

Did you enjoy it?
你鍾唔鍾意?
Nei5 zung1 m4 zung1 ji3?

That was a good book.
本書幾好。
Bun2 syu1 gei2 hou2.

Vocabulary 詞彙 ci4 wui6

Library	圖書館	Tou4 syu1 gun2
Board books	翻翻書	Faan1 faan1 syu1
Comic book	漫畫書	Maan6 waa2 syu1

22. AT THE PARK

喺公園

HAI2 GUNG1 JYUN2

Let's go to the park.	我哋去公園玩吓。 Ngo5 dei6 heoi3 gung1 jyun2 waan2 haa5.
Let's feed the ducks.	我哋去餵鴨仔。 Ngo5 dei6 heoi3 wai3 aap3 zai2.
What ride do you want to go on?	你想玩邊樣? Nei5 soeng2 waan2 bin1 joeng6
Careful!	小心呀! Siu2 sam1 aa3!
Don't run!	唔好跑! M4 hou2 paau2!
Look where you're going!	睇路呀! Tai2 lou6 aa3!
Wait your turn.	等陣輪到你。 Dang2 zan6 leon4 dou3 nei5.
Let them have a go.	等佢哋去先。 Dang2 keoi5 dei6 heoi3 sin1.
It's time to go home.	夠鐘返屋企啦。 Gau3 zung1 faan1 uk1 kei5 laa1.

Slide 瀡滑梯 soe4 waat6 tai1

Careful on the steps.	小心梯級。
	Siu2 sam1 tai1 kap1.
Slide down!	瀡落嚟啦!
	Seoi5 lok6 lai4 laa1!
Don't climb up the slide!	唔好爬上滑梯!
	M4 hou2 paa4 soeng5 waat6 tai1!
Wait for the other kid to move.	等其他小朋友行咗先。
	Dang2 kei4 taa1 siu2 pang4 jau5 hang4 zo2 sin1.

Climbing frame 攀爬架 paan1 paa4 gaa3

Climb one step at a time.	一次爬一級。
	Jat1 ci3 paa4 jat1 kap1.
Hold on!	捉實呀!
	Zuk1 sat6 aa3!
Wow you're really high!	嘩,你去到好高喎!
	Waa1, nei5 heoi3 dou3 hou2 gou1 wo3!
Do you need any help?	使唔使我幫手?
	Sai2 m4 sai2 ngo5 bong1 sau2?
You're too high, come down.	你爬太高喇,落返嚟。
	Nei5 paa4 taai3 gou1 laa3, lok6 faan1 lai4.

Sand pit 沙坑 saa1 haang1

Let's play in the sand!

我哋嚟玩沙！

Ngo5 dei6 lai4 waan2 saa1!

Don't eat it.

唔好食。

M4 hou2 sik6.

Don't throw it.

唔好掟。

M4 hou2 deng3.

Let's build a sandcastle.

我哋嚟堆個沙堡。

Ngo5 dei6 lai4 deoi1 go3 saa1 bou2.

Put the sand in the bucket.

將啲沙放入個水桶度。

Zoeng1 di1 saa1 fong3 jap6 go3 seoi2 tung2 dou6.

Tip it over.

翻轉佢。

Faan1 zyun3 keoi5.

Tap the bucket.

拍吓個水桶。

Paak3 haa5 go3 seoi2 tung2.

Lift the bucket up, that's it!

提起個水桶，係喇係咁喇！

Tai4 hei2 go3 seoi2 tung2, hai6 laa3 hai6 gam3 laa3!

Swings 盪韆鞦 dong6 cin1 cau1

Hold on!
捉實呀!
Zuk1 sat6 aa3!

Let me push you.
等我推你。
Dang2 ngo5 teoi1 nei5.

You're really high!
好高啊!
Hou2 gou1 aa1!

Do you want to go higher?
想唔想再飛高啲?
Soeng2 m4 soeng2 zoi3 fei1 gou1 di1?

Have you had enough?
玩夠皮未?
Waan2 gau3 pei4 mei6?

Five more minutes.
畀多五分鐘你。
Bei2 do1 ng5 fan1 zung1 nei5.

Vocabulary 詞彙 ci4 wui6

Park	公園	Gung1 jyun2
Slide	瀡滑梯	Soe4 waat6 tai1
Climbing frame	攀爬架	Paan1 paa4 gaa3
Sand pit	沙坑	Saa1 haang1
Bucket	水桶	Seoi2 tung2
Swings	盪韆鞦	Dong6 cin1 cau1

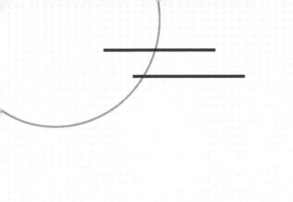

EATING

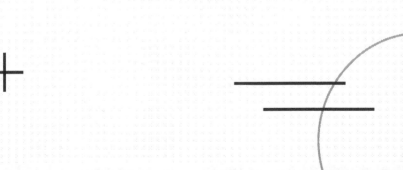

23. EATING
食嘢
SIK6 JE5

Snack time 零食時間 ling4 sik6 si4 gaan3

Are you hungry?　　　　你肚餓未?
　　　　　　　　　　　　　Nei5 tou5 ngo6 mei6?

What do you want to eat?　你想食啲咩?
　　　　　　　　　　　　　Nei5 soeng2 sik6 di1 me1?

Carrot sticks	紅蘿蔔條	Hung4 lo4 baak6 tiu4
Crackers	克力架	Hak1 lik6 gaa2
Fruit	水果	Seoi2 gwo2
Biscuit	餅乾	Beng2 gon1
Yoghurt	乳酪	Jyu5 lok3
Sandwich	三文治	Saam1 man4 zi6
Crisps	薯片	Syu4 pin2

You've had enough.　　　你食夠喇。
　　　　　　　　　　　　　Nei5 sik6 gau3 laa3.

It will be (lunch/ dinner)　就嚟食(晏/ 晚)飯喇。
soon.　　　　　　　　　Zau6 lai4 sik6 (aan3/ maan5)
　　　　　　　　　　　　　faan6 laa3.

71

It's dinner time!

食晚飯!

Sik6 maan5 faan6!

Wash your hands first.

洗咗手先。

Sai2 zo2 sau2 sin1.

Everybody, come to the table please.

大家好埋枱食飯啦。

Daai6 gaa1 hou2 maai4 toi2 sik faan6 laa1.

Let's eat!

大家食飯!

Daai6 gaa1 sik6 faan6!

It tastes delicious!

好好食!

Hou2 hou2 sik6!

Please try a bit.

試少少啦。

Si3 siu2 siu2 laa1.

You need to eat your dinner otherwise you will be hungry.

你要食晚飯呀,如果唔係陣間會肚餓

Nei5 jiu3 sik6 maan5 faan6 aa3 jyu4 gwo2 m4 hai6 zan6 gaan1 wui6 tou5 ngo6.

It's good for you!

對你有益㗎!

Deoi3 nei5 jau5 jik1 gaa3!

Would you like some more?

仲要唔要多啲?

Zung6 jiu3 m4 jiu3 do1 di1?

Have you full?

你食飽未?

Nei5 sik6 baau2 mei6?

Feeding baby /toddlers 餵BB/細蚊仔 wai3 BB/ sai3 man1 zai2

Put on a bib.	戴口水肩。 Daai3 hau2 seoi2 gin1.
Open wide!	擘大個口！ Maak3 daai6 go3 hau2!
Here comes the aeroplane!	飛機嚟啦！ Fei1 gei1 lai4 laa1!
Don't spit it out!	唔好𡁵出嚟！ M4 hou2 loe1 ceot1 lai4!
Don't drop food on the floor.	唔好跌到一地都係 M4 hou2 dit3 dou2 jat1 dei6 dou1 hai6
Well done!	好叻喎！ Hou2 lek1 wo3!

Dessert 甜品 tim4 ban2

Would you like some dessert?	你想唔想食甜品? Nei5 soeng2 m4 soeng2 sik6 tim4 ban2?
You need to eat your dinner before dessert.	食完飯至准食甜品。 Sik6 jyun4 faan6 zi3 zeon2 sik6 tim4 ban2.
Have some more dinner please.	再食多啲先。 Zoi3 sik6 do1 di1 sin1.

Drinking 飲嘢 jam2 je5

Are you thirsty?	你口唔口渴?	
	Nei5 hau2 m4 hau2 hot3?	
What do you want to drink?	你想飲啲咩?	
	Nei5 soeng2 jam2 di1 me1?	

Water	水	Seoi2
Milk	牛奶	Ngau4 naai5
Orange juice	橙汁	Caang2 zap1
Apple juice	蘋果汁	Ping4 gwo2 zap1
Cranberry juice	蔓越莓汁	Maan6 jyut6 mui4 zap
Milkshake	奶昔	Naai5 sik1
Cola	可樂	Ho2 lok6
Lemonade	檸檬水	Ning4 mung1 seoi2

Here you go.	嗱。	
	Naa4.	
Careful don't spill it.	小心唔好整瀉。	
	Siu2 sam1 m4 hou2 zing2 se3.	

Vocabulary 詞彙 ci4 wui6

Bottle	水樽	Seoi2 zeon1
Cup	杯	Bui1
Glass	玻璃	Bo1 lei1
Jug	壺	Wu4
Beaker / sippy cup	啜飲杯	Zyut3 jam2 bui1

24. GOING TO THE RESTAURANT
去餐廳
HEOI3 CAAN1 TENG1

Can I make a reservation.
我想訂一張枱。
Ngo5 soeng2 deng6 jat1 zoeng1 toi2.

Do you have a high chair?
你哋有冇高腳櫈?
Nei5 dei6 jau5 mou5 gou1 goek3 dang3?

Are there baby bottle warming facilities?
有冇BB暖奶器?
Jau5 mou5 BB nyun5 naai5 hei3?

We have a reservation.
我哋訂咗位。
Ngo5 dei6 deng6 zo2 wai6.

Can we sit somewhere else?
我哋可唔可以坐第二度?
Ngo5 dei6 ho2 m4 ho2 ji5 zo6 dai6 ji6 dou6?

Can I see the menu?
可唔可以睇吓個餐牌?
Ho2 m4 ho2 ji5 tai2 haa5 go3 caan1 paai2?

Can I see the wine list?
我可唔可以睇吓嗰酒單啊?
Ngo5 ho2 m4 ho2 ji5 tai2 haa5 go2 zau2 daan1 aa1?

Do you have an English menu?
你哋有冇提供英文餐牌?
Nei5 dei6 jau5 mou5 tai4 gung1 jing1 man2 caan1 paai2?

Is this dish spicy?	呢個餸辣唔辣？	
	Ni1 go3 sung3 laat6 m4 laat6?	
Can we have a glass of water please?	可唔可以畀杯水嚟？	
	Ho2 m4 ho2 ji5 bei2 bui1 seoi2 lai4?	
Where are the toilets?	廁所喺邊度呀？	
	Ci3 so2 hai2 bin1 dou6 aa3?	
Do you have baby changing facilities?	你哋有冇育嬰室？	
	Nei5 dei6 jau5 mou5 juk6 jing1 sat1?	
Can we get the bill please?	唔該埋單。	
	M4 goi1 maai4 daan1.	
Can we get a takeout box/ doggy bag?	打包唔該。	
	Daa2 baau1 m4 goi1.	

Vocabulary 詞彙 ci4 wui6

Menu	餐牌	Caan1 paai2
Bowl	碗	Wun2
Plate	碟	Dip6
Knife	刀	Dou1
Fork	叉	Caa1
Spoon	匙羹	Ci4 gang1
Chopstick	筷子	Faai3 zi2
Pitcher of water	一瓶水	Jat1 ping4 seoi2
Bill	埋單	Maai4 daan1

SOCIAL SKILLS & EMOTIONS

25. INTRODUCING YOURSELF

介紹自己

GAAI3 SIU6 ZI6 GEI2

What is your name?

你叫咩名?

Nei5 giu3 me1 ming4?

How old are you?

你幾多歲?

Nei5 gei2 do1 seoi3?

I am 4 years old.

我四歲。

Ngo5 sei3 seoi3.

What is your favourite colour?

你最鍾意咩顏色?

Nei5 zeoi3 zung1 ji3 me1 ngaan4 sik1?

What is your favourite toy?

你最鍾意玩邊樣玩具?

Nei5 zeoi3 zung1 ji3 waan2 bin1 joeng6 wun6 geoi6?

What is your favourite cartoon?

你最鍾意睇邊套卡通片?

Nei5 zeoi3 zung1 ji3 tai2 bin1 tou3 kaa1 tung1 pin3?

Do you have any brothers or sisters?

你有冇兄弟姊妹?

Nei5 jau5 mou5 hing1 dai6 zi2 mui6?

Do you like playing with your (brother / sister?)	你鍾唔鍾意同你啲兄弟/姊妹玩?	Nei5 zung1 m4 zung1 ji3 tung4 nei5 di1 (hing1 dai6/ zi2 mui6) waan2?
What job does your (mum / dad) do?	你(媽咪/ 爹哋)係做咩工㗎?	Nei5 (maa1 mi4/ de1 di4) hai6 zou6 me1 gung1 gaa3?
What would you like to be when you're older?	你大個想做啲咩?	Nei5 daai6 go3 soeng2 zou6 di1 me1?

Vocabulary 詞彙 ci4 wui6

Family	家庭	Gaa1 ting4
Parents	父母	Fu6 mou5
Father	爸爸	Baa4 baa1
Mother	媽媽	Maa4 maa1
Children	仔女	Zai2 neoi2
Daughter	女	Neoi2
Son	仔	Zai2
Siblings	兄弟姊妹	Hing1 dai6 zi2 mui6
Elder brother	哥哥	Go4 go1
Younger brother	弟弟	Dai6 dai6
Elder sister	姐姐	Ze4 ze1
Younger sister	妹妹	Mui6 mui6

Family tree

Mother's side

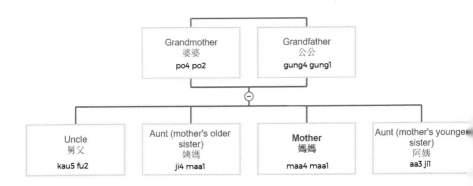

Grandmother 婆婆 po4 po2	Grandfather 公公 gung4 gung1

Uncle 舅父 kau5 fu2	Aunt (mother's older sister) 姨媽 ji4 maa1	**Mother 媽媽** maa4 maa1	Aunt (mother's younger sister) 阿姨 aa3 ji1

Father's side

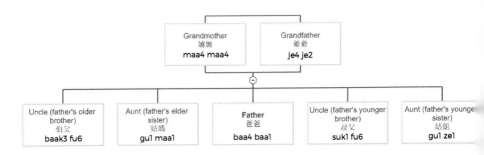

Grandmother 嫲嫲 maa4 maa4	Grandfather 爺爺 je4 je2

Uncle (father's older brother) 伯父 baak3 fu6	Aunt (father's elder sister) 姑媽 gu1 maa1	**Father 爸爸** baa4 baa1	Uncle (father's younger brother) 叔父 suk1 fu6	Aunt (father's younger sister) 姑姐 gu1 ze1

26. ANSWERING THE PHONE

聽電話

TENG1 DIN6 WAA2

Who do you want to call?	你想打俾邊個? Nei5 soeng2 daa2 bei2 bin1 go3?
Let's call grandma.	我哋打俾嫲嫲。 Ngo5 dei6 daa2 bei2 maa4 maa4.
There is no answer.	冇人聽。 Mou5 jan4 teng1.
The phone is ringing.	電話響。 Din6 waa2 hoeng2.
Answer the phone!	聽電話! Teng1 din6 waa2!
Press the green button.	撳個綠色掣。 Gam6 go3 luk6 sik1 zai3.
Say "hello."	講「哈囉」。 Gong2 "haa1 lo1".
Who is that?	係邊個嚟? Hai6 bin1 go3 lai4?
Wave to them!	同佢哋揮個手! Tung4 keoi5 dei6 fai1 go3 sau2!

I can't see you, turn your camera on.	我見唔到你，你開鏡頭吖。	
	Ngo5 gin3 m4 dou2 nei5, nei5 hoi1 geng3 tau4 aa1.	
Don't be shy!	唔使怕醜喎！	
	M4 sai2 paa3 cau2 wo3!	
Have you been a good girl/boy?	呢排有冇乖呀?	
	Ni1 paai4 jau5 mou5 gwaai1 aa3?	
Tell … what you've been up to.	話俾……知你最近做緊咩。	
	Waa6 bei2…… zi1 nei5 zeoi3 gan6 zou6 gan2 me1.	
Need to go now, say "goodbye."	要收線喇，講「拜拜」啦。	
	Jiu3 sau1 sin3 laa3, gong2 "baai1 baai3" laa1.	
Wave goodbye!	揮手拜拜啦！	
	Fai1 sau2 baai1 baai3 laa1!	
Speak soon!	遲啲再傾！	
	Ci4 di1 zoi3 king1!	

Vocabulary 詞彙 ci4 wui6

Telephone	電話	Din6 waa2
To make a phone call	打電話	Daa2 din6 waa2
Telephone number	電話號碼	Din6 waa2 hou6 maa
Video call	視像傾偈	Si6 zoeng6 king1 gai2
Hang up	收線	Sau1 sin3
Voicemail	留言信箱	Lau4 jin4 seon3 soeng

27. TAKING A PHOTO
影相
JING2 SOENG2

Let me take a picture.	等我影張相。 Dang2 ngo5 jing2 zoeng1 soeng1.
Smile!	笑！ Siu3!
Say cheese!	笑吓，cheese！ Siu3 haa5, cheese!
Look at the camera.	望鏡頭。 Mong6 geng3 tau4.
Stay still.	唔好郁。 M4 hou2 juk1.
Let me take another picture.	等我影多張。 Dang2 ngo5 jing2 do1 zoeng1.
I'm recording a video.	我錄緊影。 Ngo5 luk6 gan2 jing2.
Great photo!	張相影得好好！ Zoeng1 soeng1 jing2 dak1 hou2 hou2!

Do you want to see the picture?	你要唔要睇吓張相？ Nei5 jiu3 m4 jiu3 tai2 haa5 zoeng1 soeng1?	
Let's take a selfie!	我哋嚟張自拍！ Ngo5 dei6 lai4 zoeng1 zi6 paak3!	
That's a funny picture!	張相好搞笑！ Zoeng1 soeng1 hou2 gaau2 siu3!	

Vocabulary 詞彙 ci4 wui6

Photo	相	Soeng1
Photo album	相簿	Soeng1 bou6
To take a photo	影相	Jing2 soeng2
Photo frame	相架	Soeng2 gaa2

28. HAPPY BIRTHDAY!

生日快樂!

SAANG1 JAT6 FAAI3 LOK6!

Happy birthday!	生日快樂! Saang1 jat6 faai3 lok6!
You are now ... years old.	你......歲喇。 Nei5...... seoi3 laa3.
You are growing up so fast!	你大得真係快! Nei5 daai6 dak1 zan1 hai6 faai3!
Can you come downstairs? I have something special for you.	你可唔可以落嚟? 我有啲特別嘢送俾你。 Nei5 ho2 m4 ho2 ji5 lok6 lai4? Ngo5 jau5 di1 dak6 bit6 je5 sung3 bei2 nei5.
This present is for you.	份禮物係送畀你嘅。 Fan6 lai5 mat6 hai6 sung3 bei2 nei5 ge3.
(I/We) hope you like it!	(我/我哋)希望你鍾意啦! (Ngo5/ ngo5 dei6) hei1 mong6 nei5 zung1 ji3 laa1!
Let's put the candles on the cake.	我哋插啲蠟燭上蛋糕囉。 Ngo5 dei6 caap3 di1 laap6 zuk1 soeng6 daan6 gou1 lo1.

Let's sing Happy Birthday!	我哋嚟唱返首生日歌!	Ngo5 dei6 lai4 coeng3 faan1 sau2 saang1 jat6 go1!
Make a wish.	許個願吖。	Heoi2 go3 jyun6 aa1.
Blow the candles.	快吹蠟燭。	Faai3 ceoi1 laap6 zuk1.
Let's cut the cake.	我哋切蛋糕。	Ngo5 dei6 cit3 daan6 gou1.

Vocabulary 詞彙 ci4 wui6

Birthday party	生日會	Saang1 jat6 wui2
Birthday cake	生日蛋糕	Saang1 jat6 daan6 gou1
Birthday card	生日卡	Saang1 jat6 kaa1/kaat1
Present/gift	禮物	Lai5 mat6
Candle	蠟燭	Llaap6 zuk1
Balloon	氣球	Hei3 kau4

29. MANNERS
禮貌
LAI5 MAAU6

Excuse me.	請問	Cing2 man6 *(to get attention)*
	唔該	M4 goi1 *(to get past)*
	失陪	Sat1 pui4 *(when leaving for a while)*

Sorry. 對唔住。
Deoi3 m4 zyu6.

Please. 唔該。
M4 goi1.

Thank you.	多謝	Do1 ze6 *(for something given)*
	唔該	M4 goi1 *(for a service)*

You're welcome. 唔駛.
M4 sai2.

Please ask before taking. 問聲先好拎。
Man6 seng1 sin1 hou2 ling1.

Don't snatch! 唔好搶!
M4 hou2 coeng2!

Say "thankyou." 講「多謝」。
Gong2 "do1 ze6".

30. DISCIPLINE
紀律
GEI2 LEOT6

Be quiet.	靜啲。 Zing6 di1.
Stop!	停! Ting4!
Don't go!	唔好去! M4 hou2 heoi3!
Go!	去! Heoi3!
Stay there!	企喺度! Kei5 hai2 dou6!
Behave.	乖啲啦。 Gwaai1 di1 laa1.
I'm going to count to 3!	我數到三。 Ngo5 sou3 dou3 saam1.
I'm not kidding.	我唔係講笑呀。 Ngo5 m4 hai6 gong2 siu3 aa3.

I said no.

我話唔得。

Ngo5 waa6 m4 dak1.

Please do not touch.

唔准掂。

M4 zeon2 dim6.

Listen to me.

聽我講。

Teng1 ngo5 gong2.

Do you understand?

你明唔明?

Nei5 ming4 m4 ming4?

Apologise to ...

向……道歉。

Hoeng3…… dou6 hip3.

31. WHAT'S WRONG?
發生咩事?
FAAT3 SANG1 ME1 SI6?

Hey, what's the matter?

喂，發生咩事?

Wai3, faat3 sang1 me1 si6?

Do you want to talk about it?

你想唔想同我傾吓?

Nei5 soeng2 m4 soeng2 tung4 ngo5 king1 haa5?

I'm listening.

我聽緊。

Ngo5 teng1 gan2.

It's okay, I won't be mad.

唔緊要，我唔會嬲。

M4 gan2 jiu3, ngo5 m4 wui5 nau1

You can trust me.

你可以信我。

Nei5 ho2 ji5 seon3 ngo5.

Talk to me.

同我講。

Tung4 ngo5 gong2.

It's good to talk.

講出嚟會好啲。

Gong2 ceot1 lai4 wui6 hou2 di1.

Don't worry.	唔使擔心，冇事㗎。	
	M4 sai2 daam1 sam1, mou5 si6 gaa3.	
I'm always here for you.	我會一直喺你身邊。	
	Ngo5 wui6 jat1 zik6 hai2 nei5 san1 bin1.	

Vocabulary 詞彙 ci4 wui6

Emotions	情緒	Cing4 seoi5
Happy	開心	Hoi1 sam1
Sad	唔開心	M4 hoi1 sam1
Excited	興奮	Hing1 fan5
Calm	平靜	Ping4 zing6
Scared	好驚	Hou2 geng1
Angry	好嬲	Hou2 nau1
Silly	傻更更	So4 gang1 gang1
Embarressed	尷尬	Gaam3 gaai3
Jealous	妒忌	Dou3 gei6
Worried	擔心	Daam1 sam1

32. I LOVE YOU
我錫晒你
NGO5 SEK3 SAAI3 NEI5

I love you.

我錫晒你。

Ngo5 sek3 saai3 nei5.

Let me give you a hug.

俾我攬吓你。

Bei2 ngo5 laam5 haa5 nei5.

Give me a kiss!

錫錫我!

Sek3 sek3 ngo5!

You're so cute!

你好得意!

Nei5 hou2 dak1 ji3!

You make me so happy.

你氹得我好開心。

Nei5 tam3 dak1 ngo5 hou2 hoi1 sam

We are so happy.

我地好開心。

Ngo5 dei6 hou2 hoi1 sam1.

Mummy and daddy love you so much.

媽咪爹哋都好愛你。

Maa1 mi4 de1 di4 dou1 hou2 oi3 nei!

I'll always love you.

我會永遠愛你。

Ngo5 wui6 wing5 jyun5 oi3 nei5.

Don't worry. 唔使擔心，冇事㗎。

M4 sai2 daam1 sam1, mou5 si6 gaa3.

I'm proud of you. 我為你感到驕傲。

Ngo5 wai4 nei5 gam2 dou3 giu1 ngou6.

Vocabulary 詞彙 ci4 wui6

To cuddle/hold	攬住	Laam5 zyu6
Kiss	錫	Sek3
Love	愛	Oi3

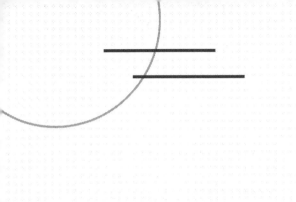

SLEEPING

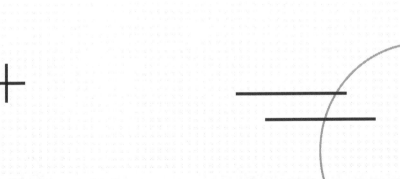

33. TAKING A NAP
瞓晏覺
FAN3 AAN3 GAAU3

Lie down with (mummy/daddy).

同(媽咪/爹哋)一齊瞓低。
Tung4 (maa1 mi4/ de1 di4) jat1 cai4 fan3 dai1.

Close your eyes and go to sleep.

合埋眼瞓覺。
Hap6 maai4 ngaan5 fan3 gaau3.

Do you want your blankie?

你要唔要安撫巾?
Nei5 jiu3 m4 jiu3 on1 fu2 gan1?

I'll be back in a bit.

我好快返。
Ngo5 hou2 faai3 faan1.

Be good and lie down.

乖乖哋瞓。
Gwaai1 gwaai1 dei2 fan3.

Vocabulary 詞彙 ci4 wui6

To take a nap	瞓晏覺	Fan3 aan3 gaau3
Blankie	安撫巾	On1 fu2 gan1
Dummy	奶嘴	Naai5 zeoi2

34. GOODNIGHT
晚安
MAAN5 ON1

Go to bed.	去瞓覺。 Heoi3 fan3 gaau3.
Are you sleepy?	眼唔眼瞓? Ngaan5 m4 ngaan5 fan3?
Hop into bed.	上床啦。 Soeng5 cong4 laa1.
Be good and stay in your bed tonight.	今晚乖乖哋喺床瞓。 Gam1 maan5 gwaai1 gwaai1 dei2 hai2 cong4 fan3.
Sweet dreams.	祝你有個好夢。 Zuk1 nei5 jau5 go3 hou2 mung6
Lights out!	熄燈! Sik1 dang1!
Love you.	錫晒你。 Sek3 saai3 nei5.
Sleep tight!	瞓個好覺! Fan3 go3 hou2 gaau3!
I'll keep the night light on.	我會開住盞夜燈。 Ngo5 wui6 hoi1 zyu6 zaan2 je6 dang1.

I can't sleep! 我瞓唔著! ngo5 fan3 m4 zoek3!

Get back into bed!

好返上床喇!
Hou2 faan1 soeng5 cong4 laa3!

No messing around.

唔好搞搞震喇。
M4 hou2 gaau2 gaau2 zan3 laa3.

I can hear you talking, be quiet!

我聽到你講嘢,安靜!
Ngo5 teng1 dou2 nei5 gong2 je5, on1 zing6!

You should sleep in your bed.

你要返去自己張床到瞓。
Nei5 jiu3 faan1 heoi3 zi6 gei2 zoeng1 cong4 dou3 fan3.

I will stay with you for a bit.

我陪你一陣。
Ngo5 pui4 nei5 jat1 zan6.

Don't wake your brother/sister up.

唔好嘈醒你兄弟/姊妹。
M4 hou2 cou4 sing2 nei5 hing1 dai6/ zi2 mui6.

Calm down.

冷靜啲。
Laang5 zing6 di1.

(Mummy/ daddy) is tired!

媽咪/爹哋劫喇!
(Maa1 mi4/ de1) di4 gui6 laa3!

Do you want me to sing you a lullaby?	要唔要我唱首催眠曲?
	Jiu3 m4 jiu3 ngo5 coeng3 sau2 ceoi1 min4 kuk1?
It's okay, I'm here.	冇事冇事，有我喺度呀。
	Mou5 si6 mou5 si6, jau5 ngo5 hai2 dou6 aa3.

Vocabulary 詞彙 ci4 wui6

Bedroom	睡房	Seoi6 fong2
Bed	床	Cong4
Pillow	枕頭	Zam2 tau4
Quilt/blanket	被	Pei5
Bedsheet	被單	Pei5 daan1
Nightmare	惡夢	Ok3 mung6
Sleepy	好眼瞓	Hou2 ngaan5 fan3
Sleep	瞓覺	Fan3 gaau3
Sleepless	冇覺好瞓	Mou5 gaau3 hou2 fan3
To oversleep	瞓過籠	Fan3 gwo3 lung4
Lullaby	催眠曲	Ceoi1 min4 kuk1

Thank you for purchasing this book!

If you have found this book useful please leave a review!

www.amazon.com/author/mooliprint

USA	Canada	UK

For any questions or suggestions please contact us at
mooliprint@outlook.com

For other books please visit www.mooliprint.com

Other books available

Made in the USA
Middletown, DE
25 September 2023

39371552R00057